Mediocrity Never Wins

The Entrepreneur's Guide to Achieving Big Profitable Results by Thinking Big

Omar Johnson

I0462551

Table of Contents

Introduction

Let's get one thing made perfectly clear right from the start here, shall we? There are essentially two kinds of business people in the world today: small thinkers and big thinkers.

Which are you?

If you immediately jump right on up there to the 'big thinker' bandwagon, you should know that there's not a lot of room up here. It's a small space and there are plenty of people all clamoring for their 'piece of the pie.' If you're even the least bit skeptical about whether or not you are really a big thinker, then you should hop back off for a minute.

It's okay, it's not the end of the road for you. In fact, unless you already think big when it comes to business, then your journey hasn't yet begun. There's still plenty of time for you to catch this ride. You might have to just walk along beside it, follow behind it, or watch from a distance until you get that 'think big' mentality ingrained within you.

You see, thinking big is not a part-time venture. It's not something that you can just sort of get along with; it's an idea, a concept, a deeply rooted sense of wanting to achieve the biggest goals in life, in your business, and not settling for second place.

Tiger Woods is one of the greatest golfers in the history of the sport, and while he has won more than anyone else in the game, he has come in second plenty of times as well. He doesn't care for second best. He says that when you finish second (and people are telling you how great you did), you're just "first loser," according to him.

Do you want to continue to be the 'first loser' when it comes to your business? Do you want to settle for just 'good enough?'

I hope not, but if you do, that's okay, too. It's just that this book isn't going to do much to help you out. You're not going to glean too much useful or valuable information from these pages. This book isn't for people who are content with 'good enough' or coming in second.

It's for people who want the best, who aim for the top, and for those who believe that what they have to offer the world is worth something special.

The strengths of thinking big

Let me ask you something: if the United States focused on just making it to space during the Space Race with the Soviet Union, do you think they would have made it to the moon?

No. They thought big. They focused on the big goals, their chance to shine. They looked to the moon and anything less was going to be a failure. And you know what? They made it.

You need to focus on the big things, the big picture. You need to set yourself up for achieving big goals. If you don't, then you're simply (subconsciously) telling yourself that you're either not good enough, worthy enough, or able to work hard enough to achieve them.

When you think small, or you think timid, then you're going to always act that way. Timid actions mean that you don't have faith in yourself or your business.

Timidity is contagious, too. It's good to be cautious for some things, but when you're too cautious, you'll lag so far behind the rest of the competition that you won't even see them in front of your for long.

Think about a cop chasing a criminal through the city streets on foot. If the criminal throws caution to the wind and doesn't really worry too much about what's ahead of him, then he's going to gain ground on the cop who has to stop at every corner to make sure a gun isn't trained on him.

You want to be the one leading the way, plotting out the best path to success, and aiming for the finish line.

So if you're still reading this at this point, that means you're ready to move beyond mediocrity and get to a place where you can move into the winner's circle for a change.

Now doesn't that just feel better? Of course it does. And you know what? Winning is contagious, too.

Chapter 1: Where Are You?

Where are you right now? No, I'm not talking about where you're sitting, standing, or whether you're on the train reading this while you're heading to work.

I'm talking about where are you within your mind? When it comes to your business, what kind of mindset do you have?

It doesn't matter whether you're just starting your new business or you've been operating it for a few years; your mindset is important. It's going to have an impact on the rest of your life, including how well your business succeeds, grows, and reaches any of the goals you've set for it.

Have you set any goals yet? Maybe your primary goal is to make it to the next year. Now that we've turned the corner into a new year, that could mean surviving all the way until the next holidays season so that you can capitalize on the surge of customers that you might get during that time of year.

Beyond that, though, do you have any real, concrete goals? If so, great. What are they? If not, then why not?

Your mindset right now will determine whether you're settling for that mediocre business or you're aiming for the moon. So let's try and determine where you are right now in your mind. It really doesn't matter whether you've actually started your new business or it's been operating for a few years.

What do you consider successful when it comes to your business? How do you measure success? Is it by the week? Month? Year? Is success just managing to break even? Do you use financial revenue as your guide?

If you're focusing only on the bottom line, then how can you move yourself closer to getting to the success you want? You won't have any concrete measuring sticks to determine where your business is at.

Are you focused solely on finding ways to get a few new customers or clients to your business every month? Is that enough?

The most important aspect of determining where your mind is at the moment is to be honest with yourself. If you're afraid of investing more time or money into your business, then you're settling for 'hoping not to fail.' Your mindset is one of timidity and hope rather than ambition and careful planning.

It's important to begin to change your mindset to be one in which you settle for nothing less than the best. In order to excel beyond mediocrity, you absolutely must begin to focus on achieving the best that you can, working for those big, lofty goals, and setting your sights much higher than you used to.

Where are you with your business right now? If you've been operating for a year, then you have some idea about how much success you have had (or lack) to this point. Don't hide from failures, though. It's easy to not want to think about all of those missed opportunities or the months that you spent on the learning curve, making costly mistakes.

It's necessary to face the things that happened and own them. If you don't, you'll always be hiding from them in the future. When you do that, you invite mediocrity to come through the front door.

What are you thinking about for the future?

Do you have a solid foundation upon which to gauge the future of your business? Where do you see your business in a month? A year? Two years? Five?

If you haven't taken the time to really think about it, then what have you been doing?

Sadly, too many entrepreneurs are actually entrepreneur wannabes. They see the opportunity with online businesses that don't have a lot of startup costs, so there's low risk. It's unfortunate because these same people don't take the entire aspect of starting or owning a business seriously enough.

They sit down one day and, lured by the prospect of being a 'business owner,' they set out to see what they could do. Their mindset is one of caution from the start. They're not going to spend too much money on this business because they truly don't know where it will lead.

They end up thinking, 'If this thing begins to take off, then I'll get serious about it.'

Do you honestly think that will work out? Probably not. In fact, more than 95% of these business 'ventures' don't last beyond six months and most of them end up sitting there, collecting the electrical dust that the Internet kicks up within a couple of weeks.

If you're thinking about the future of your business in terms of 'if ... then', stop it right now.

It's *never* going to work for you. The goal should be to achieve *profits*, not hope that you make a few sales. In order to achieve profits, you need to set yourself up as a winner from the start.

In other words, you absolutely *must* begin to think about your business, and the future, in terms of high expectations and high goals.

Determine where your mindset is

I'll be honest with you … it's not always easy to be honest with yourself. But when it comes to your business and your mindset with regard to that business, it's essential.

Figure out, honestly, where your mindset is and whether or not you have what it takes to think big, aim big, and go after the big goals.

It's okay if you realize that you don't. This can save you a great deal of time, frustration, and money in the long run.

If you don't have a big picture mindset, and you want one, then you will need to begin to develop it. Going about that can seem like a challenge, especially considering that so much of what we do as adults was ingrained in us since we were children.

But it's actually possible to 'teach an old dog new tricks.' No, I'm not calling you an old dog, or any dog for that matter. I'm just stating that it's entirely possible to mold a new mindset *when you want to*.

Chapter 2: Develop Big Picture Thinking

What was it about your childhood that you've carried with you into adulthood and is causing you to think small? Was it something that you learned? Can you pinpoint the reason for your timidity today?

For many of us, small thinking, or cautious thinking, when it comes to business was developed during our formative years. It usually wasn't something that was hard and fast, or one moment in time, but a progression of situations that built over time.

Maybe you heard phrases like, "Money doesn't grow on trees" or "Rich people are just greedy." The latter we hear almost every single day in the news media right now.

It's harmful because, for the most part, it's simply not true. Rich people tend to be driven and they *think big*. Whereas the majority of people think small.

However, those comments that you might have been surrounded with when you were younger can have a dramatic impact on the rest of your life. You might be wary of being successful because you think it's wrong. You think that earning a lot of money or having a powerfully successful business is going to lead your family to think less of you.

You might have a guilty conscience when it comes to success. Or you might be afraid of success.

People who make a lot of money without putting a lot of work in, without struggling for years to earn it (like movies stars and other celebrities) have one thing in common: guilt. They feel guilty about the ease of their success, so they think it's important to spread the message that the rich shouldn't have all that they have (yet they don't ever seem willing to part with their own wealth).

And thus the message continues to be reinforced today. I call it the *money blueprint* and it has a powerful impact on your mindset.

You likely have a habit of thinking small based on past mistakes and failures or the aforementioned lessons that you learned while growing up or watching the news. People warn us not to jump into things without thinking about them carefully.

"Are you sure that's a good idea?" your mother might say.

"What if you fail?" could be your best friend's words.

They're everywhere and when you pile them on top of thoughts about your past failures, they can compound the problem, causing you to think small.

Think small, be small.

It's time to break out of that mindset and begin to think big. Now, saying this is easy.

Doing it is much more difficult. So how do we do it?

By once again being honest with yourself.

What are your goals for your business? I'm not talking about short-term goals, but where, if you had one wish to tell a genie about your business, would you like to see your business in 10 or 20 years?

Do you hope to generate a $40,000 a year profit with your business? If so, how much time per week do you want to be working in order to earn that? 40 hours?

You might as well find a job with a major corporation. You would then get some health benefits, sick pay, vacation time, and other perks.

That's small thinking.

What about $100,000. Again, why bother? It's fine if that's what you really hope for, but that's just mediocre thinking. Not what this book is about.

Me, I think big. I think like those multi-billion dollar companies with IPOs and shareholders and a board of directors. Every business venture I take on, whether it's a brick and mortar store or online enterprise begins with that mindset.

I'm *not* afraid of the potential for success, or for failure.

Mediocrity will *not* win the race. It's that simple.

Changing your mindset is simple: it only takes a commitment. If you're willing to change your mindset, if you're tired of settling for second place or 'just good enough,' then simply repeat to yourself, 'I'm ready for the *big time* success.'

'I want to own a *multi-million* (or multi-billion) dollar company.'

'I am *going* to build my business into a major corporation.'

Now, imagine what it will be like in 10 years when you've achieved your goals.

How amazing will that be? Just think what you could do with a business that generates millions, or *billions*, of dollars every year in revenue!

Just keep repeating this mantra. Eventually your mind will accept it as reality, overwriting all of those years of mediocre

thinking.

Now, doesn't that feel great?

Chapter 3: Focused Thinking

Now that you've begun to alter your thought processes, now you're ready to get into more focused thinking.

How you think and what you focus on are just as important as having a positive and powerful mindset. Sure, you can imagine that you're the CEO of a major, multi-billion dollar company in ten years, but if you don't focus on the here and now, and get close and personal to the finer details about what you need to do in order to achieve that goal, then all you're going to be doing between now and then is daydreaming.

This is where so many people get lost.

They get caught up in imagining the major goals, the end result. They keep picturing themselves with that plush, top-floor office with the expansive views of downtown, the secretaries who are ready to wait on them hand and foot, and a thousand employees all hoping for a chance to meet the big boss, the man in charge, the one who built this company from the ground up.

Hey! Let's get back to reality.

Focus. Focus. Focus.

Realtors have a mantra that they continually talk about when it comes to helping businesses find the right places to operate. It's basically three things that are absolutely essential to have when you choose the right place for your business.

Location, location, location.

Here, it's focus.

In order to achieve the big picture, you need to focus on the small details. And every little detail is going to make a big difference in the grand scheme of your business.

A business leader who is focused on the details will tend to have a powerful force to work with.

Do you know whether your business would operate better as an online only business or will you need some form of a brick and mortar presence? I'm not talking about whether you work out of your home office because any online business has to be operated on from somewhere, usually home for most people (that's also one of the reasons many online endeavors fail … it's not easy to take a business venture seriously when you're in your pajamas or sweatpants all day long).

If you need a physical presence, then where would be ideal for it? Will it matter whether you're easy to find? Will your business require high traffic areas to be noticed?

What about the number of employees that you're going to need to start with?

Licensing and regulations.

Target audience.

And so much more. When you are aware of the details, you will be able to take charge of your business in a more efficient and effective manner.

What are your projections for investment and revenue? Per week? Per month? Per year?

Do you have any clue about how much it's going to cost you to operate your business on a weekly basis? Do you know how much it will cost per month? How long do you calculate it will take you before you turn a profit? Or until your revenue at least matches up with your expenses?

Every detail is going to be significant in the beginning.

Will you need to buy equipment? If so, could you save money buying used? Could you downsize or scale down what you might need to make it work for now? Could you outsource some of the work to save money?

When you focus on the details, you'll begin to see how you'll be able to scale and grow your business.

But it requires you to get focused and not just think about where you want to be in 10 or 20 years. If you want to think big, that's the right idea. Now it's time to focus on the small details.

The World Series isn't won by the final swing of the bat in game 7. It's won with the focus on each and every pitch from the beginning of the season through to that defining moment.

In other words, pay attention to all of the steps that you need to take right now that will put you on the path toward long-term, viable success.

When you do that, you're going to also need to get all of the little details worked out.

Let's talk about getting some financing, hiring the right employees, the pitfalls of hiring, things to think about when considering taking on partners, and a few other factors that matter when it comes to business.

You know, those pesky yet important details.

Chapter 4: Line Up the Details

In order to get focused, you need to have a good bead on the details. It's all of those small, seemingly insignificant aspects of running a business that, while you may not want to bother with them later when you're generating millions of dollars a year, are important right here, right now.

Take a look at some of the more important details when it comes to this new business venture of yours. Do you know where you'll operate your business? What about employees?

Of course, how about the most important aspect of the beginnings of any business … money?

Let's start with finances.

Get your financing in order

It doesn't matter whether you're looking at starting an affiliate marketing business in the few spare hours a week that you have, or you're planning on going in full-bore with a new store in town, or whether you already started your business. You absolutely must have your finances in order if you want to be successful.

A lot of business advice will tell you that you should keep your personal and business finances separate. Yes, this is true. However, there are some exceptions to this rule and I will get into them shortly.

The best thing that you can do for yourself and your new business is to do everything that you can to avoid getting into heavy debt from the beginning. Yes, you may need to get into *some* debt, but don't rely on it to get you through the tough times, especially if you have the opportunity to pay off some of the debts that you incurred in the beginning of this venture.

Too often, what we're taught growing up about money is either just plain wrong or we didn't learn much of anything.

Work with cash as much as you can. Now, this is where I differ from some of those financial gurus who tell you to keep your personal finances separate from your new business endeavor.

If you have savings, then this is where you should begin when trying to finance your business. A lot of people will say, "But I don't want to risk losing my savings. Why would I want to tap into my *personal* savings for this?"

It's simple. It's there. You're not earning a lot of money from it sitting in a savings account. Right now, the average savings account is earning an annual rate of less than 1 percent. That's not going to help you with long-term anything, so why wouldn't you want to invest it in something that could lead to long-term wealth?

Another aspect about relying on your personal savings to help fund your new business is that if you're holding back because you worry about losing it, then you're not fully invested emotionally in your business. You're expecting it to fail.

When you expect something to fail, then you won't give your full effort. You won't really be trying your best, will you? I doubt it. The thousands of failed business owners who held back, who worried about failing will tell you the same thing. The only way to truly improve the chances of being successful is to go all in.

You can think about it in terms of poker. The best players in the world are the best, and remain that way for one simple reason: they know when to bet big. Does that mean they always win those hands? No. It only means that they know what to look for and when the opportunity arrives for them to bet it all, they go for it.

Your business is your royal flush and when you focus on the details and understand what you need to do in order to succeed, you're going to improve the odds of success. By holding back and worrying about 'what if' then you're not really going to be fully invested in it.

The world will see the bluff for what it is and you will lose.

So don't shy away from tapping into your savings. This will have a number of side benefits for you as well.

1. You won't have to rely on anyone else for money. Forget asking family or friends for a loan. If you don't pay them back in time, it could cause hard feelings. Also, someone who loans you money may feel

that it gives them a right to tell you how to do certain things with your business. You don't need that.

2. You don't start out in debt. That's always a positive. Avoid getting into debt as much as possible. If you have to, then pay off your debts *as soon as* you can. Don't wait and hold onto the money *in case* something goes wrong.

3. It will cause you to be more detail oriented and *committed* to your business. When you are putting your own savings on the line, you're going to work extra hard to protect it, to make sure that it has the best opportunity to succeed and bring in a strong return on your investment.

What about investors? You can certainly take on investors, but there are two basic kinds: angel investors and venture capitalists. We'll get into these in more details in Chapter 6: Partnerships Can Go a Long Way, but before you take on any investors, understand what they expect to get from the arrangement.

Crowd funding is another option that you can look into as well. This is where you find people who believe in your business venture enough to make a small (or significant) investment in it. In return, they would generally get something out of the deal.

For example, if you're planning on building a new device that could be used for computers, but you need financial backing to create it, your crowd funding investors could get some of the first prototypes for their investment, or a set of them, depending on the criteria.

These are just a few options to consider.

Now, what about employees?

When you're ready to hire employees, you want to choose the *right* ones from the outset. Try to avoid hiring friends or family members, unless they are gifted and can bring something incredibly special to your business.

You want to have employees who can help boost your business. You're not running a charity event here, so don't feel bad if your best friend, who has been out of work for three years and spending most of his days playing Call of Duty on the Xbox comes by asking for a job. If he doesn't have the skills, knowledge, or network power to help you company grow, without you being a mentor and babysitter in the process, then politely decline.

Once your business is booming, then you can consider taking him on as an employee, if you want.

Make your hiring decisions wisely. Think about each person you hire as an *investment* in your business. Ask yourself some key questions when interviewing them:

1. How can they help improve your business?

2. What do they bring to the table that you don't have right now?

3. Will they need a lot of hand holding? If so, then they're probably not ideal for your business. Right now.

4. Are they eager enough to work for you?

5. Will they buy into your long-term goals?

6. Are they **Big Thinkers** like yourself? If not, keep looking.

Keep in mind that it will cost, on average, $16,000 to hire each new employee, based on national averages. That includes the time to search for them, interview all of those applicants, and then train them properly. It could take up to 6 months before they are fully integrated into the business.

The smaller your business is in the beginning, then less this will cost, but when you think about *each hire* as an investment of this sort, you'll be more likely to hire the right ones for your business.

Now, let's talk about execution.

Chapter 5: Execute

What does the word execute mean? I'm not referring to the textbook definition, but rather what it means to you.

Does it mean that you're going to have some plans in place and then just sort of toss them out the window at the first sign of trouble? Just because something is not working for you the way that you planned doesn't mean the idea was flawed. It would more likely be that the *execution* was flawed.

So what does it really mean to you? Well, whatever it is, if it's different than the following, then you need to take some time and truly think about it again.

Execution means taking your plan and putting it in action.

It's about taking the plays that you came up with in the locker room at half time and actually doing them on the field. Think you can do that?

It's not always as easy as it sounds. There are a million things that can go wrong between the planning stage and execution. Your employees might not fully understand what you're trying to do and they may not ask questions. A mistake could be made and if adjustments are not made in time, they could cause the whole plan to fall apart.

But just because things *can* go wrong, that doesn't mean that they *will*. You can increase the odds of things going according to plan by having detail plans from the beginning, by thinking about every contingency, by contemplating the things that can go wrong as well as the things that can go right.

Do you play chess? If not, you should try it. The game has been around for centuries and continues to be incredibly popular. It's a thinking man's (and woman's) game and the best players plan ten, fifteen, or even more moves *ahead* of time. They anticipate what their attack strategy is and what their opponent is going to do. And even though you might have the next fifteen moves planned in your head, if your opponent does something that you don't expect, it could require you to completely change your next fifteen moves.

The goal is still the same: capture the king and win the game while avoiding a stalemate.

So make your plan, but even at that point it's not enough. You also need to know *how* to execute.

The reason why so many businesses fail is because the owners don't really know how to execute.

Have you ever heard of the difference between a 'manager' and a 'leader?' Managers basically just keep things moving forward. They don't possess great people skills, don't really understand leadership, and are more prone to disciplining people for things that didn't go right rather than mentoring to help them learn and grow.

Managers take the directive from their bosses and hand out assignments. Leaders inspire. Leaders execute.

There are plenty of resources out there that can help you learn how to become a leader for your business. It doesn't need a manager, it needs a captain.

If you drop a ship in the middle of the ocean without a captain, do you think it will reach its destination? Not likely.

Learn how to execute and all of that hard work planning everything will become more powerful.

Speed and launching a business

When is the right time to launch this business or get this new product idea out to the marketplace? If you're waiting for the spring, or summer, or maybe even just heading into the next Christmas shopping season, then you're missing a lot of opportunities.

The best time to launch your business is *right now*.

It doesn't matter what the business is. When you launch it right now, you're going to be that much closer to achieving success.

Just consider this: two people plan to walk across the country for charity. One decides to take off on New Year's day. There's a storm coming, so the second decides to wait. Two weeks after New Year's, the second is still waiting for the weather to be 'ideal' for them to head out. They don't want to get caught by snow or cold winds or even rain. So they wait.

Within six months, the first person reaches the opposite coast and her charity receives a ton of money. The second one just took off. The weather's finally warm enough, but he's going to have trouble raising money like the first one because it was just done.

He waited too long.

Just because you launch right now, that doesn't mean that everything is perfect, that every plan is refined. Speed is more important than perfectionism when it comes to your business in the beginning.

It's like the novelist who keeps rewriting and editing instead of sending the manuscript out to agents and publishers. It's just an excuse to avoid the risk.

If you're going to think big, you need to also *act big*, which means getting your business *launched*. When it comes to that, there's no time like the present.

What are you waiting for? I'll wait right here. Go ... get it started!

Chapter 6: Partnerships Can Go a Long Way

When you're starting out your new business, you might feel as though you're shipwrecked on an island with no other land in sight. You don't even know where you are, so you wouldn't know where to begin to figure out what direction to face.

You could head west, only to realize that California was just forty miles to the east and nothing but four thousand miles of open ocean in front of you.

But that doesn't mean that you *are* alone. You can consider taking on partners, but it can be a tricky situation.

As I mentioned in Chapter 4, there are investors and partnerships that can benefit you, especially when you're looking for some extra cash to get your business off the ground.

Angel investors are people who can provide some capital for a startup business. Usually, though, they want a piece of the equity. This could mean giving up 10 percent or more of your profits, or less, depending on the investment.

These arrangements can be short-term or long-term, though someone who is going to invest in a business is going to be thinking more about long-term returns. Don't expect to buy someone off with a few percentage points in profit sharing for a year or two.

Some of these angel investors are going to want to have some active role in the business.

This can create some problems, especially if they don't understand your target market, the products you're offering, or the services that you'll provide. If you don't want this person to have an active role, then decline their offered investment.

Venture capitalists tend to deal in millions of dollars and they tend to be high risk, high reward endeavors. Unless you're a multi-million dollar business owner that has established a powerful presence and success already, don't expect to find a venture capitalist looking in your direction.

If you're looking for someone to be a partner, then they will make some kind of investment in the business, like you. This could be financial or it could be their hard work.

A partner should be someone with whom you can get along. If your personalities clash, this can cause trouble for the business. Sure, some tension can be useful, but that usually only applies to creative aspects.

When it comes to the core of your business, make sure that you will be able to get along with and work with this other person.

There's no limit to how many partners that you have on board, but whether you choose one or five, have well-defined roles and expectations. You don't want one person suddenly trying to dictate how to run your office when their role is in shipping, for example.

It's best to have every partnership formal. Don't take on a friend as a partner as this is usually a recipe for a broken friendship and lawsuits. Get everything documented and signed. Any question that either of you may have about the partnership should be detailed in writing, and signed. You can usually design contracts and agreements between you, but if you feel that it's important to be legally protected, then hire a lawyer to lay the groundwork.

Have an *ironclad prenup*. Just like some wealthy men and women have prenuptial agreements to protect themselves in the event of a divorce, it's a good idea to have them for your business. If things don't go well with your partner, if you both agree that it's time to sever the partnership, you can avoid losing half of your business, and then facing a new competitor right there, next door, by having a prenup.

It's your business, you invited him or her to join. You should retain that business. There will certainly be stipulations, though. You can't expect to take advantage of another person's hard work and then not pay them anything when you force them out.

A business prenuptial should be designed by a lawyer and it should be fully agreed upon by all parties before being signed. If something doesn't sit well with anyone, then they shouldn't sign.

Finally, have an *exit strategy* for each partner. Know how long they plan on being a partner in the business and what their buy out share will be in advance, assuming that the business follows the goals and plans.

The more detail you can put into your partnership plans and strategies, the better it will be for everyone involved, especially your business.

Partners should be as dedicated and invested in your business and its success as you are. If they aren't, then they could end up being a liability, or just dead weight. If that's the case, then it's time to cut them loose or don't even bother with them from the beginning.

There are plenty of people out there who would be interested in partnering with you. Just make sure that they bring something to the table that you don't yet have. It could be experience, creativity, or even connections. The more holes you fill with partners, the more well-rounded your business will become.

Chapter 7: Location, Location, Location

Another topic I touched on earlier was location. Well, in reality I only mentioned it as something that Realtors will like to tell you when it comes to *where* you should open your business, or buy a house. In those terms, location is everything.

Buy a great business and set it up in the part of town that is dark, where the roads are still gravel and not highly traveled, and you'll probably not have many customers coming out to you.

Set up shop in the center of town where thousands of people wander by every day and you're likely going to be much more successful.

However, location means it will cost you more, so you're going to need to temper your desire to be in the heart of all the action with the need to save some money.

Finding the balance can be tricky for new business owners.

What if your business is online?

That doesn't change a thing. You're going to still need to think about location, location, location. However, when it's on the Internet, it's about *positioning, positioning, positioning*.

You want people to be able to find your company website. If they can't find it, then what good is it doing?

I heard an analogy about websites some years ago and it still rings true today. If you build a website, but no one can find it through a search engine and you don't market it, then it's like building a store in the middle of the woods with no roads that get to it. You might have a straggler wandering through the woods find it, but that's about it.

You need to think about positioning your online presence and that means getting on the first page of search rankings.

Search Engine Optimization is a massive industry today, and for good reason. More than **90 percent** of all first-time visits to a website are generated through a search engine. That means that nine out of every 10 people who find your website will do so through a search engine like Google, Bing, Yahoo, or any of the others.

Google is still the king, accounting for a 62 percent share of all global searches. That's massive. That's also why most SEO experts focus their energies on algorithms that Google *most likely* uses to rank websites.

That means that you will need to know three essential components of your business. First, you'll need to know your target market. If you assume that you're targeting anyone with a pulse, you're already planning to fail.

Males, 18-25. Elderly women, 65-75. Professional men and women, 40-50.

Those are targets. Those are focused demographics. You need to understand your target market. That doesn't mean that you won't have 58 females purchasing your products that are targeting 18-25 year old males. However, if 60-70 percent of your customers are going to be the latter, then don't advertise to attract the former. Instead, accept that as an added bonus. If you find that there's another strong market later on, you can build a new marketing campaign targeting just them.

The wrong business in the right place can sometimes be successful. You don't want to be lucky, though ... you want to be *good.*

Second, you need to understand your products or services. If you don't understand them, how can you sell them? If you need to learn about these products, get down and dirty and learn everything you can about them. Why do they work? Why would people want them?

What makes them better than others? Quality? Durability? Price?

If you offer services, how are they different than your competitors? What sets you apart? Again, dig into them to uncover these finer details.

Third, you need to become an expert in the field. Give information. Presence online or in the real world if amplified when you can impart valuable information to others.

Teach people how to use your products. Offer free seminars or classes that extoll the benefits of them. Become an authority on the topics.

All of these will help you with both a brick and mortar based business as well as an online-only presence. When you position yourself

properly, you'll be able to take full advantage of

location, location, location.

Chapter 8: Customers Are the Lifeblood of Any Business

I don't care how you try to slice it or wriggle out of it, the fact still remains … customers are the lifeblood of any business.

Now, don't give me that nonsense that you don't really have 'customers.' Maybe you offer consulting services to corporations. Maybe you supply maintenance to Internet service providers. Maybe you drive a truck.

You know what? Every single one of those business have *customers*. Just because they may be nameless, faceless people who write checks to you and schedule all of their actions or have all of the interactions conducted online via email, that doesn't mean they aren't customers.

If you sell products or services (the only two things that you *can* sell), then you have customers.

And customers are the lifeblood of any business. That's not something that you can get around. And it is absolutely essential that you understand this and make every interaction with your customers count.

Think about this: a company spends $1,000 a month on marketing. Their efforts generate 40 leads (40 people who find their ads interesting enough to check out what the business actually has to offer). That means each *lead* costs $1,000 divided by 40, or $25.

Now, out of those 40, 10 decide to buy something from the business. That means ¼ of the initial interested customers actually buy something. So, if you now divide $1,000 by 10, you get an investment of $100 for *each new customer*.

If you generate $750 in sales from those 10 new customers, you're losing money.

A lot of money.

However, what if the business owner focused on building **relationships** instead of reeling in customers? If the marketing campaign was a bit different, if the responses to inquiries or the website or the store was cleaner or more professional looking, then he or she might have gotten **100 interested people** to stop by and take a look (as opposed to the original 40).

Then the initial investment would be $1,000 divided by 100, or $10 (as opposed to the original $25).

Then, if the business focused on building relationships, maybe 50 of those 100 purchased items and bought $5,000 worth of merchandise. That's a *profit*.

But it's not over. If you begin building relationships, those same customers could end up coming back time and time again, boosting sales to $10,000, $20,000 or more, *all for that single marketing campaign*.

How you treat your customers, from the very beginning of the interaction, is how you will build long-term success. Marketing is fine, but you need to have some way to bring in the people who find your business, to make them feel comfortable, to set yourself apart from other businesses. It's not enough to just act as though these interactions are impersonal.

People are longing for more personal interactions with businesses these days. They get plenty of the lousy customer service when they go to their local supermarket or Home Depot or Wal-Mart or just about anywhere in the malls these days.

They *long* for something more. They want to feel as though they matter.

That's where you can win. And win ***huge!***

Focus on ways to build relationships. This doesn't mean you have to wine and dine them, but when they contact you by email or call you on the phone, don't pass them off as though they're not really all that important. Make them believe that they are important.

Respond in a timely manner. Get their name, remember it, and use it.

"You know what Michelle, I understand completely what you're talking about."

"Mike, I'm so glad you brought that to my attention."

"We'd like to show our appreciation to you Sara, so this is what I'm going to do …"

Pay attention to them when they have something to tell you. Listen to them. While there are plenty of customers who are just going to complain about anything and everything that they can, that doesn't mean they're wrong.

You can pay attention to them, but just remember the Pareto Principle that states 20 percent of your customers can consume 80 percent of your resources (time). At the same time, 80 percent of your revenue will be generated by 20 percent of your customers.

Recognize which ones are which and focus your energies on that 20 percent that generates the majority of your revenue. Forget those that consume your resources.

Reward loyalty. What good is it going to do you when you spend all of your resources trying to impress and make happy those customers who aren't going to come back anyway? Let them go.

Reward those who come back to you time and time again.

Be creative, too, when rewarding those who are loyal. Of the utmost importance, though, is building those relationships. It's never too early or late to start doing so, either.

Speaking of creativity …

Chapter 9: Be Creative

Doing what everyone else is doing, or doing things the same way as your competition is not the way to win.

Remember, this is all about winning. You can't think *big* if you're not thinking about winning. NFL teams don't think about anything *but* winning the Super Bowl. Sure, there are seasons where some teams need to focus on building a better offensive line, or a better special teams, or getting the quarterback who is going to lead them to the championship. However, the ultimate goal is to *win*.

As it should be for you and your business. If you're not planning on winning, then what are you doing all of this for in the first place?

So how do you get there? How do you defeat your competitors and impress the customers?

You do it by thinking creatively. Sure, there are plenty of things that will work that are traditional, tried and true, and tested. And they are fine for some aspects of your business.

But what about getting more attention? What about getting people to stop and take notice?

You want people to first *know* about your business. Once they know about it, they will be more inclined to pay attention to it.

There are countless ways to conduct business, market, serve customers, design products, commit to service, find ways to improve customer care, save money, and the list goes on and on.

The only way to do things that haven't been done before, to do things that are unique and can work for you, is to be creative.

What does it mean to be creative?

It's about 'thinking ahead.'

Look to the future and 'see' what's in store. Get a solid understanding of where your business (and other businesses) are right now, where technology might take us, and focus on capitalizing on that power as soon as you can.

Star Trek is one of the most successful television and movie franchises in history. It has a strong and loyal following and you know what? If you look at some of the earliest episodes with

William Shatner as Captain Kirk, pay attention to their communication devices. They look an awful lot like the simple flip phones that were popular when cell phones first became practical for the average consumer.

There are dozens of ideas that the series spurred into reality, all because the creators were *creative*.

Are you going to come up with the next amazing revolution in communication? Who knows? You just might. But that's not the point.

The point is that you need to embrace creativity.

Too many business owners try to stifle creativity. They view it as being too risky. That's because they don't fully understand it. They believe that by allowing their employees to be creative, they are going to detract from productivity and thus lose revenue in the long run. So while their humming along contentedly, their main competitors come up with the ideas that catapult them far ahead, leaving that antiquated business scrambling to catch up.

When it comes to scrambling to catch up, eventually winning becomes a product of chance, rather than planning.

Get in the habit of encouraging creativity. Allow your employees, partners, and teams to come up with some new ideas for dealing with different situations. This could simply be how a product is marketed or in how customer interactions are conducted. Whatever it is, listen to and pay attention to those new ideas.

That doesn't mean that you have to accept any of their ideas, but the more you listen to them, the more you inspire even *more* creativity and that can lead to the winning idea that catapults you above and beyond your competitors.

How do you encourage it?

First, let your employees, or your team, know the importance of being creative. Let them know that you want them to come up with different ways of doing things, but that it's not enough just to have an idea … they also need to determine how it will improve the business, ways to implement it, and cost factors.

You can actually serve two purposes by having a once-a-month lunch meeting where you encourage everyone to share their ideas. You can also provide a box to submit ideas for people who are a bit shy about them. Read them openly at the meeting and when people talk about them, you can see if there's any substance to this creative idea.

Often, the best ideas are created through a brainstorming process.

The GUI interface that we have become accustomed to with regard to computers (those icons that you click on to open programs) was actually developed first as a means to teach children how to use computers. It eventually was realized that adults would benefit from that system as well and, well, the rest is history.

There needs to be a balance with regard to creativity and creative energy. The ideas should flow, but they should be within reason. If you allow too much room to roam for your team, then they could end up spending too much time and too many resources *trying* to be creative.

Also, the idea of having a state of the art communication system installed in the office that could cost you ten thousand dollars or more is not realistic.

You just never know where the next great idea is going to come from and if you stifle creativity, though, you can be sure you'll know where it's *not* going to come from.

3M created Velcro when one of its employees was home and walking through the brush in the woods outside his home. He ended up having all these burrs stuck to him and the light bulb clicked on. Of course, his idea netted the company millions and he didn't get anything from it.

You'll be fairer to your employees, though, if they come up with a revolutionary idea, right? Of course you will.

Chapter 10: Think Like a Big Business

How many employees do you have, or will you need when you start your new business? Is it just going to be you in the beginning? Or will you have a team of people working with you?

In all honesty, it doesn't really matter and you want to know why?

Because no matter the size of your business, you need to think about it like it's a big business.

What does that mean?

More importantly, is that always a good thing?

Okay, it depends on what we're referring to when it comes to thinking like a big business.

For big businesses, loss is an acceptable thing.
They know that there's going to be what's known
as 'shrinkage' in business, whether from
shoplifting, internal theft, or breakage. There's
also going to be loss when it comes to items that
can't be sold, or have to be discounted heavily in
order to get if off the shelves.

Whether you want to have an 'acceptable'
threshold for loss within your business is up to
you. I personally don't accept any losses, though
I know they're going to happen. I'm certainly not
going to punish an employee for accidentally
dropping the iPad they use for work, but I am
going to be more careful about who gets what.
When it comes to internal theft, there's no
acceptable threshold as far as I'm concerned,
though. You steal from me, you're fired. And

then some. If I can prove it, you're going to be charged.

Too many companies, in my opinion, are too lax when it comes to theft. They fire the employee when it's discovered, but if it's minor (meaning small dollar amounts), they don't pursue charges. That doesn't send a clear and strong enough message to the rest of the team. Of course, if you build your team properly, you won't have to worry about it, anyway. Who's going to want to steal from their teammates?

One thing that big businesses do very well is run major operations. They have complex systems that are designed to smooth the flow of information and they have departments that are responsible for very specific tasks.

We can learn a lot from these systems. They have a CEO or President, then vice president and managers, then team leaders, middle management and all the way down to the entry level employees.

They pay attention to the finer details. They promote employees who excel, who are driven, and who are determined to help the company succeed. They know when to let other employees go as well.

They have human resource professionals who understand just what kind of employees will make the best ones and they work diligently to get them on board when they find them during the interviewing process. Remember when I said that it costs, on average, $16,000 to hire and train a new employee? That's why these big companies take their time making sure they get the best one.

The more time it takes to fill a position, and the more appropriately a person is compensated, the better the retention.

Focus on retention of employees through benefits, bonuses, and more. It works for those big companies.

All of the finer details matter when it comes to your business and while you may be overwhelmed with things that have to get done, that doesn't mean you can or should just ignore them.

If you can't pay attention to them, you should hire someone who can. Yes, another employee to pay can cut into your profits, but there's only so much potential when you're running the show all by yourself.

Marketing

Another aspect that big businesses do well is *marketing*. Every small business could learn a thing or two from big businesses when it comes to marketing.

Sure, we don't have the massive multi-million dollar budgets that can compete with those big businesses, or throw money away like they do. Just look at the *millions of dollars* that some of the largest companies in the world spend for a 60 second ad during the Super Bowl! There are simply no measurement devices in place to determine if those ads boost sales or not. Yes, they experiment, but they also do a lot of research to find out just what their *target market* is using and how they find information about new products and services that they may be interested in.

Pay attention to those details. If your business is similar to a major corporation's operations, then see where they advertise. Do they have a social media presence? Do they get involved in interacting with customers? Can you find blogs about it somewhere? If so, do you notice a trend with the comments left on those blogs?

There could be a few great opportunities for your business to capitalize on them.

Marketing is key to business success. If you don't think that you have the resources to advertise and market, if you don't think it's all that important, then you're not thinking big.

It's not about throwing your money away. It's about generating new customers. Don't just pay $50 to run a small ad in the local paper that 20 people might read. Dig into the details and test your marketing strategies. If you don't know how to test them, hire a consultant, or better yet … *brainstorm* with your team.

Hey, you just might find some incredibly new and exciting ideas that are ***big!***

If you want to ***be*** big, you need to ***think*** big.

Chapter 11: Guerilla Warfare

Alright, now we're getting pretty serious here. Now we're getting into war and war is a very serious business.

No, we're not talking about picking up arms and charging an enemy on some distant field, hoping that we don't take a hit and go down in a blaze of glory. (Now that those clichés are done, we can move on.)

We're talking about efficient ways of engaging the enemy.

If you stood 5 foot 5 and weighed 120 pounds soaking wet and you were facing down a giant of a man who stood well over 7 feet and weighed in at better than 370 pounds of pure muscle, you'd probably do best to avoid him.

However, if you're going to compete against him for a million dollar prize, and knocking out your opponent was the goal, how would you even *think* about winning?

If you're not suicidal, you certainly wouldn't go head to head with this guy. Even if you were a master of martial arts, you're still at a disadvantage in sheer size, weight, and strength.

No, you'd have to rely on your quickness. Your speed at maneuvering could be an advantage, depending on the field of battle. You can move quicker while your opponent would lumber. By the time he moved one of those massive arms to hit or grab you, you could strike and be behind him, striking again.

Guerilla warfare isn't about fighting dirty, but rather using the resources that you have, that give you an advantage over your opponent, and using them against your opponent.

We've grown accustomed to hearing about guerilla warfare as being similar to terrorism, but it's much larger than that. The American Revolution was won by guerilla warfare tactics. The British Army was far stronger and more superior, so the patriot rebels would lure the British into dense spaces, such as forests, and would then strike from cover. They also focused on taking out senior officers which, until that time, was an unwritten rule that you don't target officers. Without officers leading the ranks, the British Army fell apart; they didn't know what to do.

Was that dirty or effective? I suppose it all depends on which side you are fighting on.

Guerilla warfare defies brute strength. Major corporations move slow. When a new technology or media strategy is developed that can put businesses in touch with customers, it could take months or even years for a major corporation to catch on or agree to get on board. Smaller businesses can take advantage of these new technologies because decisions can be made quicker.

Blogging, social media, and other recent innovations on the Internet have helped smaller businesses snag a larger share of revenue from those corporations that don't get involved with them at all, or quickly enough.

If you're going to run your business in the modern world, while you should think like a big business, you can't go up against one. If you charge that giant, all the screaming and roaring that you do isn't going to mean much when he wraps his big, thick arms around you and breaks your back.

You need to use the tools and resources that you have available to try and strike hard and fast and then move onto the next battlefield.

Determining *what* those strategies will be and where the battlefield are will be up to you. The big companies won't care; they don't spend any time thinking about you. For now.

When you're big enough to be noticed, it's already going to be too late for them to adjust.

Business is war. War is ugly. Don't be lured in by the sense of respect or that younger generations today don't respect the older ways of doing things. That's just an excuse to lose.

Business is about survival and evolution. Those who are willing and able to change and especially those that are creative and can *create* the future are the ones that are going to make the most of it.

It's time to accept your role as the little soldier standing in the midst of all those giants. You don't need to attack them all. Just grab a few pounds of flesh from a few here and there and you'll soon be grabbing the customers that they neglect. It'll be a small percentage to them and they won't be looking at you as a reason for their losses; they'll only be looking at the bottom line numbers and them trimming their workforce when they keep losing.

In the meantime, thanks to your guerilla style warfare, you'll be on your way to becoming one of those big businesses.

Conclusion

Think small. Be small.

It's a mantra that many professional athletes rely on. It's also one that some business owners agree with.

When you think small, you're only going to be planning on small things happening for your business. You'll develop habits that only generate minor results. While that may be fine for you, if you took the time to read this entire book, I'm just going to assume that's not the case.

This book has been about *thinking* big because you want to *be* big.

You've been thinking about this business for some time, or you've been operating it for a while and still don't have anything to show for it … yet.

That's probably because you've been hunkered down in the confines of mediocrity. It's easy to get lost in there, though. You're not alone if that's what happened.

All of those years that you were told to 'play it safe,' 'why don't you find a good job for a major corporation,' or 'avoid taking too many chances,' you began to believe in the inherent nature of the message, which is: accept mediocrity.

Yet the biggest businesses in the country and around the world did *not* accept mediocrity.

They went after the brass ring, the Holy Grail, the ultimate prize. The founders of those companies had bigger visions in store for their companies.

Colonel Sanders didn't start out thinking that he was going to just sell some chicken because people really liked the recipe. He wanted to sell *a lot* of chicken. He knew that a new interstate was going to be running through town and decided to buy a piece of land right at the exit. He didn't go in the center of town; he knew there would only be a limited number of customers who would buy his chicken.

He thought *big*. He wanted to grab all of those passers-by on the highway and he did.

Today, his company is one of the largest fast food chains in the world.

The Waltons didn't think they would be the biggest retailer in the world when they started; they wanted to deliver exceptional service and low prices to their customers. Eventually it became Wal-Mart.

You don't win when you don't think you can win. If you're not willing to think big, if you honestly don't believe that you have what it takes to be big, then that's fine. Just go into your business venture understanding that you'll always be one small slip up from going out of business.

However, if you're ready to take charge and you know that you have the ability to be big and to make it big in the world of business, then it all starts by altering your way of thinking. Changing our way of thinking, especially when it's been ingrained in us for many years, is a tough road, but it all starts with a simple choice.

The choice is: what do you *really* want? Do you want a big, successful business or a small, struggling one?

If you still want the big one, then change your thinking, and follow the advice in this book and you'll be on your way!

If you need further assistance I offer one on one coaching through my Entrepreneur Mentorship Program. For more information and a Free Consultation just visit:

http://www.makeprofitseasy.com

Good luck and I wish you much success with your entrepreneurial endeavors.

Sincerely,

Omar Johnson

Other Books Available By Author On Kindle, Audio and Paperback

Crushing The Competition: The Entrepreneur's Guide To Using Military Strategies To Outthink, Outmaneuver and Outperform The Competition

How To Transform Yourself From Employee To Online Entrepreneur: Escaping The 9 To 5 Wage Slave Syndrome

Money Talks Bullshit Walks: The Entrepreneur's Guide to Productivity and Making More Money By Eliminating Distractions, Time Thieves and People Who Are Full of Shit

The Killer Instinct: How To Master It and Achieve Anything That You Want

Winning Habits: Getting Rid of A Loser's Mentality

Conquering Your Fears

Passive Income: Stop Working Hard For Your Money And Let Your Money Work Hard For You

How To Create A Profitable Ezine From Scratch

The Secrets Of Making $10,000 on Ebay in 30 Days

The Complete Guide To Investing in Gold And Silver: Surviving The Great Economic Depression

How To Sell Any Product Online:"Secrets of The Killer Sales Letter"

Smart Money: How To Get Out Of The Consumer Trap And Invest Your Money Wisely

How To Make A Fortune Using The Public Domain

Search Engine Domination: The Ultimate Secrets To Increasing Your Website's Visibility And Making A Ton Of Cash

Creative Real Estate Investing Strategies And Tips

How to Make Money Online:"The Savvy Entrepreneur's Guide To Financial Freedom"

How to Overcome Your Self-Limiting Beliefs & Achieve Anything You Want

The Secrets of Finding The Perfect Ghostwriter For Your Book

The Creative Real Estate Marketing Equation: Motivated Sellers + Motivated Buyers = $

How To Start An Online Business With Less Than $200

How To Market Your Business Online and Offline

Money Blueprint: The Secrets To Creating Instant Wealth

Affiliate Cash: How To Make Money As An Affiliate Marketer

How To Promote Market And Sell Your Kindle Book

AudioBook Profits: How To Make Money by Turning Your Kindle, Paperback and Hardcover Book into Audio.

The Fine Art of Writing The Next Best Seller on Kindle

Fast Cash: 9 Amazing Ways To Make Money Without Having To Work At A Job

Money Magnet: How to use the Laws of the Universe to Attract Money into Your Life

Hypnotic Influence: How To Create A Cult Like Following For Anything That You Do

The Art of Manipulation: How to Get Anybody to Do What You Want

Jobless Cash: How to Make Money if You're Unemployed or Just Plain Tired of Working for Someone Else

What They Didn't Teach You In School About Money